Jams and Jellies

Homeworld

The Publisher:
Lone Pine Publishing
#206, 10426-81 Avenue
Edmonton, Alberta, Canada
T6E 1X5

Canadian Cataloguing in Publication Data
   Jams and jellies

   (Homeworld)
   ISBN 0-919433-90-1

   1. Jam. 2. Fruit—Preservation. I. Series.
TX612.J3J34 1990   641.8'52   C90-091499-8

Editorial: Phillip R. Kennedy, Debra Rebryna, Doug Elves
Research: Keith Ashwell
Cover Design: Beata Kurpinski
Cover Photo: Yuet Chan
Printing: Friesen Printers. Altona, Manitoba, Canada

The publisher gratefully acknowledges the assistance of the Federal Department of Communications, Alberta Culture and Multiculturalism and the Alberta Foundation for the Arts in the production of this book

Contents

Introduction

Jams and Jellies is both a comprehensive handbook for the beginning jam maker and a useful collection of recipes for more experienced cooks. This book does not rely on complicated, high-tech processes or chemical additives, but is about those time-tested methods used by our parents and grandparents to stock their kitchen cupboards. It contains easy step-by-step directions for making jams, jellies, marmalades and preserves with everyday kitchen utensils and supplies. Special sections on freezer jams and jellies are also included in the recipes. For quick reference, a metric conversion table and a glossary with detailed entries for important technical terms can be found at the end of the book.

It is certainly easier to get commercial jams and jellies from the supermarket. Preserving fruits at home, however, guarantees additive-free jams and jellies made from the freshest ingredients. Exciting combinations of flavours can be tried at home and new concoctions savoured; such unique preserves are an excellent gift for special occasions.

Making jams and jellies is also an economical way to store fruits for the coming year; fruit bought in bulk is ideal for processing in large quantities, and home-grown produce adds a personal touch to preserves. The possibilities are endless.

Before You Begin

A Kitchen Checklist

The organized preserving kitchen should have:

- One or two large pans, (2 to 4 L) for boiling the fruit, sugar and water
- One canner, preferably aluminum, copper or enamel-finished, with a tight-fitting lid and a wire basket for holding the jars in place. A canner should be large enough to allow for 3 cm of water below the jars and 5 cm of water above them.
- One or more colanders, for draining fresh-washed fruits and fruits that have been blanched for easier peeling
- A kitchen scale, preferably metric
- A candy thermometer
- Sugar
- Commercial pectin, liquid or powdered
- Wax paper
- Paraffin wax
- Sterilized home canning jars
- Cheesecloth or a jelly bag for making jellies

Buying In Bulk

While it is always worthwhile to take advantage of the sale of fresh fruits in bulk, market conditions can never be guaranteed to last for a definite length of time and quantities vary, from region to region. However, the following is a general guide to what fresh fruits are currently available in bulk.

Apricots: Sold in "volume fill" 7 kg cases

Berries: Sold in 12-by-1 pint packs

Blueberries: Sold in 5 lb. and 10 lb. bulk packs

Cherries: Sold loose in 18 to 20 lb. boxes

Kiwis: This native of New Zealand is occasionally available in 12 lb. trays, sold according to size.

Oranges: Sold in 40 lb. loose-pack cartons, in 15 lb. consolidated-pack cartons and in 4 lb. and 8 lb. boxes and bags.

Peaches: Sold in volume-fill 24 lb. packs and in trade-wrapped 16 lb. Panta-Paks (trade containers contain individually wrapped or separated fruit).

Pears: Sold in trade-wrapped 45 lb. cases and in 17 lb. Handi-pack volume-fill cases.

Plums: Sold in 24 to 26 lb. volume-fill packs.

Prunes: Sold in 24 to 26 lb. volume-fill packs.

Strawberries: Sold in flats of 12 individual 1-pint baskets.

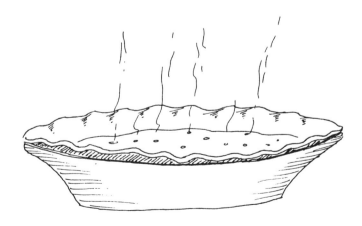

Containers

Most brands of canning jars (Mason jars) are composed of three distinct parts: the glass jar itself, a screw-top ring and the flat metal lid. Wash the jars thoroughly and sterilize them with boiling water before using them, no matter how clean they look. It is not safe to assume that the jars will be sufficiently sterilized when they are immersed in a hot-water bath during processing. Lids must also be sterilized.

Canning Jars

Old screw-top rings may be used over and over again, provided that they are in good condition and hold lids securely in place. Never re-use old lids, however. The sealing compound along their rims is only effective once; they will not safely seal again. Always buy a new set of lids for each new batch of jams or preserves.

Additionally, any jar which is going to receive hot preserves should be warmed beforehand to prevent shattering.

Some older jars (Bell jars) with glass lids may still be in circulation. If this type of container is to be used, be sure to replace the disposable rubber ring which makes a seal between the lid and the jar.

Jam jars come in a number of sizes.

Canning jars are commonly available in the following range of sizes:

Imperial	Metric
1/2 pint	284 mL
1 pint	570 mL
1 quart	1,130 mL
2 quarts	2260 mL

Any recipe that involves sterilizing in hot water baths or putting very hot mixtures into jars should not employ "recycled" store jars. For such recipes use commercial home canning containers that are made from appropriately tempered glass and have seal caps and screw tops that will ensure an impenetrable seal. Other cold-process preserves can be stored in commercial jam and pickle jars.

Go through a checklist of all possible kitchen requirements before going to a supermarket or farmer's market to buy your fruits or vegetables in quantity or in bulk. The essence of good results is the freshness of the produce in the first place. Valuable time can be lost if you suddenly have to chase down a stray cheesecloth or a hidden thermometer.

Packing and Processing

Frequently in this book you will come across the phrases "hot pack" and "cold pack." Both terms refer to the preserve's temperature during bottling. Hot-packed jams or fruits are cooked before canning; cold-packed fruits are merely preserved with syrup. The best fruit for cold-packing is tomatoes, because they hold their shape. In general, hot packing results in more fruit by volume and less liquid.

Processing

For proper processing it is very important that the bottles or jars do not rest on the bottom of the canner, and that the canner is deep enough to allow for at least 5 cm of hot water to cover the contents.

The canner should be half filled with water and brought almost to boiling point before the jars, in the canner's basket, are lowered into the water. The jars must not touch.

The jars should be filled to the level of headspace (see Glossary) designated in the recipe. Before the jar is sealed, run a knife or a spatula around the sides of the jar to remove any air bubbles trapped in the mixture. The lids should be tightened, and then loosened slightly to allow the release of air during heating. Cover the jars with sufficient hot water, but do not pour a pan or kettle of hot water directly on to the jars: the heat could crack the glass. Bring the water to a rolling boil. This is the moment when the processing time begins. It is important not to extend the time indicated in the recipe, as the preserve's flavour or texture may be changed by over-cooking.

Then, using tongs, a heavy kitchen towel or kitchen mitts remove the jars. Set them on a cookie rack or even a thickness of tea towels or newspapers and allow the jars to begin cooling. As soon as the latent heat has stopped cooking the preserves, the jars should be sealed as tightly as possible.

When the jars are completely cool, tip them and leave them upside down or on their sides overnight to check the quality of the seal. If some liquid oozes out from under the lid, or the lid bulges, the seal is not perfectly airtight. The preserves should then be eaten or thrown out.

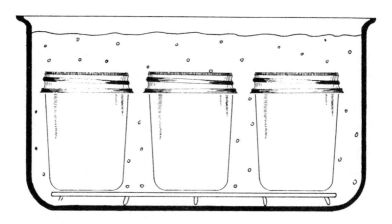

A Canner or Canning Kettle

Making Syrups

The following syrup table is a guide: jam makers and fruit preservers tend to either refine or add their own signature to their product as they become more experienced.

Very light:
250 ml sugar, 750 ml water to make 875 ml syrup
Thin:
250 ml sugar, 500 ml water to make 625 ml syrup
Moderately thin:
250 ml sugar, 400 ml water to make 525 ml syrup
Medium:
250 ml sugar, 250 ml water to make 375 ml syrup
Heavy:
250 ml sugar, 200 ml water to make 325 ml syrup

To make syrup, mix sugar and water and stir constantly until the mixture comes to a boil. The syrup should be boiling hot when poured over the fruit. In a " hot pack," the jar can first be half-filled with syrup and fruit, briefly simmered and then topped off with fruit and boiling syrup.

Selected Recipes

Preserves

The word "preserve" can apply to any food processed for long-term storage: jams, jellies, relishes, even pickles. This chapter is concerned with a narrower meaning; that is, fruits stored in a sugar syrup for future use.

Virtually any fruits available in your local supermarket or food store can be bottled using the procedures below as a general guide. Sweet fruits will usually require lighter syrups than more sour ones.

Apples

Tart, Granny Smith apples can be saved for use in pies and pastries; sweeter apples are best for purées and sauces.

Peel, slice and core apples. Put the slices in salt water or an ascorbic acid solution (15 mL of ascorbic acid per 2 litres of water) until ready for canning. This will prevent them from losing their colour. Don't leave the apples in the solution for more than 20 minutes (see Glossary under "Discolouration").

Pack in jars and cover with very light syrup and seal. The syrup should be poured gradually into the jars to prevent shrinkage.

Set jars in warm water, bring to simmering point and maintain for 30 minutes.

Check seals and store.

Blackberries

Select firm berries that are almost ripe. Wash them thoroughly to remove any dirt or foreign material. Pick out the berries which are obviously under-ripe or over-ripe.

Pack in jars and cover with very light syrup to about 2.5 cm from the jar top and seal. The syrup should be poured gradually into the jars to prevent shrinkage.

Set jars in warm water, bring to simmering point and maintain for 30 minutes.

Check seals and store.

Blueberries

Wash the blueberries and remove any immature or over-ripe berries. Pack in jars and cover with a medium syrup to about 2.5 cm from the jar top and seal. The syrup should be poured gradually into the jars to prevent shrinkage.

Set jars in warm water and boil for 15 minutes.

Check seals and store.

These berries can be used in pies, dumplings and muffins.

Cherries

Use firm red or black cherries; the Bing variety is best for preserving. Wash the cherries and remove stalks and leaves. Pack in jars and gently cover with a medium syrup to about 2.5 cm from the jar top and seal.

Set the jars in warm water and boil for 15 minutes.

Check seals and store.

Peaches

Blanch and peel peaches. Halve and remove stones. Put the slices in a salt water or ascorbic acid solution (for a maximum of 20 minutes) until you are ready to can them.

Pack in sterilized jars and cover with light or moderately light syrup to about 3.5 cm from the jar top. Seal and place in boiling water for about 15 minutes. Check the seals and store.

Pears

Peel, core and quarter desert pears. Keep the quarters in a salt water or ascorbic acid solution (for a maximum of 20 minutes) until you are ready to can them.

Pack in jars in medium syrup and process for 20 minutes. Whole or powdered ginger may be added to the syrup to enhance the pears' flavour. Check the seals and store.

Plums

Wash plums, remove stalks, halve and discard stones. Put the slices in a salt water or ascorbic acid solution (for a maximum of 20 minutes) until you are ready to can them.

Place plums in a saucepan and cover with heavy syrup. Boil for 2 minutes. Pack them in sterilized jars with syrup, leaving 2.5 cm headspace. Process for 15 minutes, check seals and store.

Raspberries

These need to be washed thoroughly but gently, so that the berries do not bruise.

Hull them (remove the stalk and attached leaves).

Remove damaged, over-ripe or under-ripe fruit.

Loosely fill sterilized jars with the raspberries, cover with a medium syrup to about 2.5 cm from the jar top and process for 15 minutes.

Rhubarb

Rhubarb stalks should be topped and tailed (especially if leafy material and offshoots appear) and gently scrubbed to remove all traces of soil.

Chop the rhubarb into about 3 cm lengths. Pack into jars and cover with boiling medium syrup to about 2.5 cm from the jar top. Seal and process for 20 minutes. Check the seals and store.

Strawberries

This is another fruit that demands gentle but thorough washing, both to prevent bruising and to get rid of unwanted materials.

To remove stalks use a sharp paring knife or potato peeler. The core should come out with no effort.

Pack loosely, in sterilized containers and cover with a boiling medium syrup to about 2.5 cm from the jar top. Process for 15 minutes. Check the seals and store.

Jams

Jams are by far the easiest and safest home preserves to make. They are made of either whole or pulped fruits that are boiled with sugar and pectin. The sugar, in addition to sweetening the jam, inhibits the growth of micro-organisms and prevents fermentation; the pectin reacts with acids in the fruit and jells the mixture. In general, one kilogram of jam equals about one quart.

Apricot Jam

(Makes 2 kg)

1.3 kg fresh apricots
275 mL water
1.5 kg sugar
120 mL lemon juice

Wash and pat the apricots dry, remove any stalks, halve and remove stones. Place the apricot halves, water, sugar and lemon juice in a pan, simmer to dissolve sugar and then boil until the setting point is reached (104°C). Fill jars and seal. Stir continuously to avoid burning.

Ginger-Apple Jam

(Makes 3 kg)

2 kg cooking apples
1.4 kg sugar
750 mL water
juice and grated peels of 3 medium lemons
250 g ginger, finely chopped
5 mL ginger powder

Peel, core and slice the apples and keep them in a weak brine solution to prevent discolouration. Place the cores and peelings, which are rich in natural pectin, in a cheesecloth bag. Drain the slices and put them in a pan with the bag of peelings and the water. Simmer until the apples are completely softened.

Remove the bag and briefly purée the apple slices in a blender. Put the purée in a pan, add the sugar, ginger, ginger powder and lemon juice and peels. Simmer and stir to dissolve the sugar. Then boil until setting point has been reached (104°C). Fill jars and seal.

Sealing with Paraffin

Sealing in mason jars with new rubber seals will often be adequate for your preserves. But, including a paraffin wax seal will give you an added measure of security against spoilage.

Paraffin wax is best melted in a double boiler because it is very flammable. When pouring the first layer of wax, rock the liquid paraffin around the rim of the jar to make a complete seal. Then place a piece of kitchen string around the inner rim of the jar and cover with a second layer of wax. The free end of the string can be pulled to make the wax plug easy to remove.

Pineapple-Apricot Jam

(Makes 3.5 kg)

2 kg fresh apricots
250 mL pineapple cubes
2.3 kg sugar
120 mL lemon juice

Wash and blanch the apricots, then peel, remove stones and chop. In a large bowl combine the chopped apricots, pineapple cubes and sugar. Mix contents thoroughly and leave overnight in the refrigerator.

The next day, bring mixture to a boil and continue boiling for about 10 minutes. Then add the lemon juice and boil for a couple of more minutes, stirring continuously to prevent burning, until the desired thickness is obtained. Fill jars to within 0.6 cm of top and boil in sealed, sterilized jars for 10 minutes. Check seals and store.

(Makes 2 kg)

1.5 kg blackberries
150 mL water
1.5 kg sugar
30 mL lemon juice

Wash blackberries and discard immature or over-ripe berries. Place the blackberries, water, sugar and lemon juice in a pan and simmer to dissolve sugar. Remember to stir frequently to prevent burning. Then bring to a vigorous boil until the setting temperature (104°C) has been reached. Fill jars and seal.

(Makes 2 kg)

1 kg blackberries
1.5 kg sugar
350 g cooking apples
150 mL water

Wash blackberries and discard immature or over-ripe berries. Peel, coe and slice the cooking apples. Place the blackberries, apples, water and sugar in a suitable pan. Simmer to dissolve sugar, stirring frequently to prevent burning. Then bring to a vigorous boil until the setting temperature (104°C) has been reached. Fill jars and seal.

Blackcurrant Jam

(Makes 2 kg)

1.25 kg blackcurrants
750 mL water
1.5 kg sugar

Gently remove stalks from the blackcurrants. Remove bright-red berries, as they are unripe. Add the water and sugar to the berries. First simmer to dissolve sugar and then maintain at a vigorous boil, stirring occasionally to prevent burning, until jam reaches desired thickness. Fill jars and seal.

Imperial Cherry Jam

(Makes 2.5 kg)

1 kg ripe cherries
700 g sugar
30 mL lemon juice
15 mL salt

Sort and wash the cherries. Remove stalks and pits. A cherry pitter may be helpful for handling large quantities of cherries. Cut some of the cherries in half. Mix them thoroughly in a large bowl with the sugar, salt and lemon juice. Simmer to dissolve sugar and then bring to a vigorous boil. Stir occasionally, to prevent burning, until the setting point of 104°C is reached. Fill jars and seal.

Cranberry-Apple Jam

(Makes 2 kg)

1 kg cranberries
1.5 kg cooking apples
1.2 kg sugar
600 mL water

Sort and wash cranberries. Peel, core and slice the apples.
In a large saucepan dissolve the sugar into the required amount of water. Add cranberries and apples and bring to a brisk boil, stirring occasionally to avoid burning. Continue Boiling for about 20 minutes, until the mixture is set. Fill jars and seal.

Perfect Peach Jam

(Makes 2 kg)

1.5 kg ripe, unbruised peaches
1.5 kg sugar
275 mL water
60 mL lemon juice

Blanch (see Glossary) the peaches. Then skin and quarter them. Discard the pits. Place the peach quarters in a large pot and add the sugar, water and lemon juice. Simmer to dissolve the sugar and bring the mixture to a boil. Continue boiling for 20 minutes, until the setting point is reached. Stir constantly to prevent burning. Then fill jars and seal.

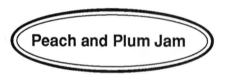

Peach and Plum Jam

(Makes 2 kg)

1 kg cooking plums
0.5 kg fresh peaches
1.5 kg sugar
275 mL water

Wash and blanch the peaches. Then skin and quarter them. Remove the stones from the plums and peaches. In a large pan combine the fruits with the sugar and water. Simmer, stirring often, and bring to a boil until the jam has set. Fill jars and seal

Plum Confiture

(Makes 2 kg)

1 kg plums
1.5 kg sugar
275 mL water

Remove stones from the plums. In a large pan combine the plums, sugar and water. Simmer, stirring often to prevent burning, and bring to a boil until the jam has set. Fill jars and seal.

Green, purple or black plums can be used for this preserve.

Raspberry Jam

(Makes 2 kg)

1.5 kg raspberries
1.5 kg sugar

Place the raspberries and sugar in a saucepan. No additional liquid is required. Heat very gently, stirring with great care. When the sugar is thoroughly dissolved bring the mixture to a boil and continue boiling and stirring until the jam has set. Fill jars and seal.

Old Fashioned Strawberry Jam

(Makes 2 kg)

1.5 kg strawberries
1.5 kg sugar
450 mL liquid pectin
50 mL lemon juice

Wash the strawberries thoroughly and remove bruised and spoiled fruit. Remove the stalk and leaves with a paring knife by pulling them away together with the pithy inner stem. Cut some of the strawberries in half to make the jam juicier.

For whole fruit jam try to select smaller berries; also, large berries can be halved. For a spread, crush the berries with a potato masher.

In a large saucepan mix the lemon juice and strawberries. Boil for 2 to 3 minutes, remove from heat and stir in the sugar and commercial pectin. Gently heat the mixture until the sugar is completely dissolved, then boil it for about 20 minutes or until the jam has set. Stir occasionally to prevent burning. Fill jars and seal with either waxed paper or paraffin wax.

Freezer Jams

For apartment dwellers and those with limited kitchen space, freezer jam represents an ideal opportunity to process fruits in quantity when the price is competitive.

Freezer jams do not require any cooking; commercial pectin helps them set. These preserves do not necessarily have to be stored in a freezer unless a considerable batch is made. Freezer jams kept in the refrigerator will last for up to three weeks.

General Directions

The basic procedure for making freezer jams is as follows:

- The fruit is run through a food processor or pulped by hand
- The liquid is carefully measured and the exact amount of sugar is added
- After stirring, appropriate quantities of pectin and lemon juice are added
- The mixture is left to stand for a short time and is then poured into jars

Freezer Jam Hints

In freezer jams, reconstituted lemon juice should be used instead of fresh lemons, as the commercial product has a standardized strength.

When making a freezer jam, always buy more fruit than indicated in the recipe. Losses in bruised or otherwise undesirable fruit, and the removal of skins, pits and peel can amount to as much as 25 percent of a bulk purchase.

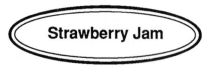

Strawberry Jam

(Makes 1.2 kg)

1 kg strawberries
1 kg sugar
1/2 bottle (9 mL) pectin
10 mL reconstituted lemon juice

Wash and core the strawberries. Then, with a potato masher mash the strawberries, a few at a time. Measure 420 mL of pulped fruit. Add sugar to the pulp. Stir thoroughly and let stand for 10 to 15 minutes. Add the pectin and lemon juice and stir for 3 to 5 minutes.

Fill jars with the jam, leaving 0.5 cm headspace. Seal tightly and leave in a warm place for 24 hours. Then freeze or refrigerate.

Raspberry Jam

(Makes 1 kg)

1.5 kg raspberries
1 kg sugar
1/2 bottle (9 mL) pectin
10 mL lemon juice

Wash the berries gently and remove any dirt, leaf particles and under- or over-ripe berries. Mash and measure 470 mL. Stir in the sugar and let stand 10 to 15 minutes. Add the pectin and lemon juice. Stir for 3 to 5 minutes.

Fill jars with the jam, leaving 0.5 cm headspace. Seal tightly and leave in a warm place for 24 hours. Then freeze or refrigerate.

Peach Jam

(Makes 1.5 kg)

1 L fresh peaches
1.5 kg sugar
one bottle (18 mL) commercial pectin
60 mL reconstituted lemon juice

Blanch the peaches for two minutes. Skin and remove stones. Chop peach halves finely or blend them in a food processor. Measure 650 mL of peaches, and stir in the sugar. Let stand 10 to 15 minutes.

Add the pectin and lemon juice, stirring for 3 to 5 minutes. Fill jars with the jam, leaving 0.5 cm headspace. Seal tightly and leave in a warm place for 24 hours. Then freeze or refrigerate.

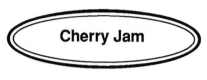

Cherry Jam

(Makes 1 kg)

500 mL Bing cherries
1 kg sugar
1/2 bottle (9 mL) commercial pectin
60 mL lemon juice

Wash and sort the cherries. Remove stems and pits (a cherry pitter may save time). Chop the cherries very finely or blend them in a food processor. Measure 420 mL of the prepared cherries and add the sugar. Stir and let stand for 3 to 5 minutes.

Add the pectin and lemon juice, stirring for 3 to 5 minutes. Fill jars with the jam, leaving 0.5 cm headspace. Seal tightly and leave in a warm place for 24 hours. Then freeze or refrigerate.

Marmalades

These are usually jams or preserves made with citrus fruits, notably oranges, lemons, limes and grapefruit. Marmalades incorporate the rind as well as the fruit, so finely shredded that during cooking they become translucent.

Lemon and Orange Marmalade

(Makes 2 kg)

450 g large, juicy oranges
250 g fresh lemons
1.5 kg sugar
1.75 L water

Peel the fruits, leaving the desired thickness of pith on the fruit. Save the peeled pith and the seeds. Squeeze the juice from the fruit and pour it into a large pan.

Now place the pulp in a blender and, after blending briefly, the resulting liquid should be poured into the pan.

The remaining pulp, pith and seeds should be wrapped in cheesecloth and tied securely.

Add the required amount of water to the juice, drop the pith bag in and simmer for at least 2 hours. By that time the liquid should be reduced by about half.

Add the sugar and allow it to dissolve. Bring the mixture to a rolling boil until the setting point is reached.

If the marmalade contains fruit peels, it is important that it be allowed to cool and form a film of jelled liquid over the surface of the jam.

If marmalade is poured into jam jars while still hot, the peels will rise to the top, leaving nothing but a clear liquid at the bottom. On the other hand, if the jam cools too much, bubbles will form.

Any citrus fruits can be used in a marmalade. A sweet edge can be introduced into a mixed marmalade by the addition of Seville oranges, tangerines or mandarins.

Rhubarb Marmalade

(Makes 2.3 kg)

6 oranges, chopped and peeled
orange peel
1 kg finely chopped rhubarb
2 kg sugar
240 mL water

Add the oranges and chopped rhubarb to the water and boil for 10 minutes. Julienne 230 mL of orange peel. Add the orange peel and sugar to the mixture and boil for 30 minutes, stirring frequently. Skim froth; allow the marmalade to partially cool. Then pour into jars and seal tightly.

Scotch Orange Marmalade

(Makes 2 kg)

8 large oranges
2 L water
2 kg sugar
240 mL lemon juice
120 mL Scotch whisky
100 g butter

Cut and quarter oranges, removing cores and seeds. Cut the coloured rind frim the withe pith and discard the pith. Briefly shred oranges with a blender. Coarsely julienne the rind and soak overnight in water.

Next day, bring the oranges to a boil and let cool. Add sugar and lemon juice and boil until the liquid reaches 104°C. Remove the pan from heat, skim as necessary, stir in the butter and Scotch. Pour into jars, close lids, and boil in a hot water bath for 5 minutes. Remove the jars, seal them and store.

Melon Marmalade

(Makes 0.5 kg)

2 large melons (preferably cantaloupes)
1 orange
1 lemon
2 kg sugar

Peel and section the melons to make melon cubes. Peel and pith orange and lemon. Shred the orange and lemon in a blender. Add melons and citrus juice to the mixture. Let stand overnight. Julienne or grate half the orange and lemon peels and add them to the mixture. Bring to a boil, stir and simmer until marmalade thickens.

Let cool and stir to mix the citrus peel. Pour into jars, close lids and process in a boiling water bath for 5 minutes. Remove, seal tightly and store.

Zucchini Marmalade

1.5 kg zucchini
4 large oranges
1 lemon
2.5 mL baking soda
2.5 kg sugar
1 bottle (18 mL) commercial fruit pectin

Peel and pith the oranges and lemon. In a food processor, coarsely chop the zucchini and the prepared fruits. Combine mixture with baking soda and sugar. Leave 1 hour. Bring to a boil and let the marmalade simmer for one hour. Remember to stir the mixture to prevent burning. Some of the orange and lemon peel may be cut into thin strips or grated and added during simmering. Remove film or froth as it develops. Remove from heat. Stir in 1 bottle of fruit pectin (18 mL - 6 oz). While still hot pour into jars and seal.

Summer Marmalade

(Makes 1 L)

2 L green tomatoes
3 lemons, peeled
1 L sugar
3 mL salt

Thinly slice the tomatoes and sprinkle salt over them. Separate the lemon peel from the pith and julienne the peel, then combine the peel and tomatoes in a large pot and add enough water to cover the mixture. Boil for ten minutes and drain.

Thinly slice the lemons, saving any juice produced. Add sugar, lemon slices and juice to the tomato mixture, and cook over low heat until the sugar melts, stirring frequently.

Let cool and stir to mix the citrus peel. Pour into jars, close lids and process in a boiling water bath for 15 minutes. Remove, cool and seal tightly and store.

Jellies

While jams and marmalades are made from chopped or crushed fruit, jellies are fruit juice preserves. Most recipes require a jelly bag to separate the juice from the pulped fruit; a simple substitute can be made with three or four pieces of cheesecloth tied at the corners. The best results are obtained with a slightly damp jelly bag (see Glossary).

Raspberry Jelly

3 L raspberries
1.8 L sugar
1 bottle (18 mL) commercial pectin

Wash and sort the berries, removing all over-ripe fruit. Crush the berries and pour them into a jelly bag, and suspend the bag over a pot or large bowl. Let drain overnight. Measure 960 mL of the prepared berry juice. Add juice and sugar to a large pot and bring the mixture to a boil. Stir frequently to prevent burning or sticking. Lower heat and add the liquid pectin. Bring to a boil again, for about a minute. Using a ladle, pour the hot mixture into sterilized jars, leaving 0.3 cm of headspace, and seal.

Grape Jelly

1.7 kg grapes
120 mL water
1.7 L sugar
1/2 bottle (9 mL) commercial pectin

Sort and wash the grapes. Remove stems and crush. Add water and boil, simmering for 10 minutes. Pour the mixture into a jelly bag, and suspend the bag over a pot or large bowl. It is important not to squeeze the jelly bag to speed up juice extraction, as the resulting liquid will make cloudy jellies. Keep the juice overnight.

The next day, pour the juice through two layers of cheesecloth; this removes any unwanted crystals. Pour 960 mL of the strained juice into a large pot and add the sugar. Bring the mixture to a boil and add the liquid pectin. Boil the mixture again for about a minute, pour the hot mixture into sterilized jars, leaving 0.3 cm of headspace, and seal.

Old-Fashioned Apple Jelly

(Makes 1 kg)

1.7 kg apples
960 L water
720 mL sugar

Wash and core apples. Cut the fruit into small pieces, placing them in a large pot. Add water and boil, simmering for about 25 to 30 minutes. Pour the mixture into a jelly bag, and suspend the bag over a pot or large bowl. Let the juice drain overnight.

The next day, add 960 mL of the juice and all the sugar to a large pot. Boil until the mixture sets. Pour the hot jelly into sterilized jars, leaving 0.3 cm of headspace.

Lemon Jelly

600 mL pasteurized honey
180 mL lemon juice
15 mL lemon rind, grated
1/2 bottle (9mL)
    commercial pectin

Combine lemon rind, honey and lemon juice and boil mixture. Add pectin and boil again for one minute, stirring constantly. Remove from heat and stir for a few minutes, then pour into sterilized glasses, leaving 0.3 cm headspace.

(Makes 750 mL)

1.2 kg cranberries
360 mL water
600 mL sugar
5 mL cinnamon
2 mL ground cloves

Discard over-ripe and under-ripe berries. Put berries and water into a pot and cook over low heat until the cranberries are soft. Process the berries in a blender, food mill or food processor. Pour the crushed berries into a pot and add the sugar, cinnamon and cloves. Cook until the mixture sets, then ladle into sterilized jars, leaving 0.3 cm of headspace, and seal.

240 mL fresh mint leaves
720 mL sugar
240 mL water
120 mL cider vinegar
1/2 bottle (9 mL) commercial pectin

Wash the mint leaves and stems carefully and put them into a pan. Crush the leaves and add sugar, water and vinegar. Boil until the sugar melts, then add the liquid pectin and boil again for about half a minute. Strain and pour into sterilized jars, leaving 0.3 cm of headspace, and seal. Green food colouring may be added to enhance the jelly's appearance; it is added to the mixture along with the pectin.

Currant Jelly

(Makes 1 L)

3 L currants
500 mL water
720 mL sugar

Thoroughly wash currants, and place in saucepan. Add water and boil, then simmer for 10 minutes. Pour the mixture into a jelly bag, and suspend the bag over a pot or large bowl. It is important not to squeeze the jelly bag to speed up juice extraction, as the resulting liquid will make cloudy jellies. Let the juice drain overnight.

Put the sugar and 960 mL of the juice into a large pot. Boil the mixture for about five minutes, stirring frequently until the mixture sets. Ladle jelly into sterilized jars with 0.3 cm of headspace and seal.

Pectin

Fruits contain varying amounts of pectin. High-pectin fruits need little or no additional pectin, while low-pectin fruits require added pectin.

High Pectin Content:
Apples, blackberries, crabapples, cranberries, lemons, plums, quinces, oranges.

Low Pectin Content:
Apricots, peaches, pears, prunes, raspberries, strawberries.

Blackberry Jelly

(Makes 2 kg)

3 L blackberries
1.8 L sugar
1 bottle (18 mL) commercial pectin
60 mL reconstituted lemon juice

Wash and sort the berries, removing all over-ripe fruit. Crush the berries and pour them into a jelly bag, and suspend the bag over a pot or large bowl. Let drain overnight. Measure 960 mL of the prepared berry juice. Add blackberry juice, lemon juice and sugar to a large pot and bring the mixture to a boil. Stir frequently to prevent burning or sticking. Lower heat and add the liquid pectin. Bring to a boil again, for about a minute. Using a ladle, pour the hot mixture into sterilized jars, leaving 0.3 cm of headspace, and seal.

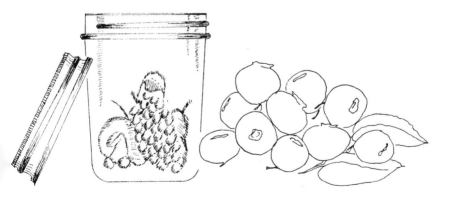

Glossary

Blanching

Blanching is a must for preserving some fruits and vegetables, as the process not only stops the ripening action of a plant's enzymes but also kills almost all potentially dangerous bacteria.

The food to be blanched is first placed in a wire basket, colander or wire skimmer, and is then lowered into a pot of boiling water for 15 to 60 seconds, depending on the size, ripeness and variety of produce you are using. The food is then quickly immersed in cold water to stop the cooking process.

Peaches, apricots and tomatoes are peeled much more easily if they have been blanched beforehand.

Discolouration

Discolouration may be displeasing to the eye, but does not affect the nutritional value or taste of the fruit. It can be prevented by briefly soaking the fruit in a brine or ascorbic acid solution (5 mL of salt or 0.5 mL of ascorbic acid powder to each litre of water).

Headspace

Headspace is the amount of space between the top of the jar and its contents. It is very important to use the recommended headspace measurement in any recipe that calls for the product to be heated in a bath of boiling water.

If the jar doesn't have enough headspace, it could explode when the contents of the jar expand. If the jar has too much, its contents may become discoloured; but worse, an airtight seal may not form, giving harmful bacteria room to breed.

Jelly Bag

This is an all purpose cloth bag used for crushing fruits. The fruits you wish to use are placed in the jelly bag and you crush the contents with your hands. The cloth acts as a strainer, letting the juice run out while containing the crushed fruit within. It is usually made from a muslin fabric and can be purchased wherever you by your preserve supplies.

Pectin

One of the mysteries of jam and jelly making, pectin is a natural substance that induces juices and pulps to jell or solidify. Fruits which contain a lot of pectin, such as apples, require little pectin for processing. Others, like strawberries, may have their pectin supplemented with commercially produced pectin. Most of the recipes in this book use bottled pectin. Pectin in pouches may be used instead; each bottle is equivalent to two pouches of pectin. If powdered pectin is used, it must be added to the fruit juice before heating, not after boiling as with liquid pectin.

Setting

The pectin in jams and jellies is activated by heat. When the fruit juice reaches a certain temperature the pectin reacts with sugar and acid to jell the mixture. There are different ways to check the setting point of such preserves. The simplest method is to spoon a little liquid into a saucer and let it cool for a few minutes. If the surface begins to wrinkle, the setting point has been reached. Some cooks put a few drops of liquid onto a wooden spoon. If the preserve falls off in a jelled sheet, the mixture is ready.

Spoilage

Spoilage is a natural stage in the growth of fruits and vegetables. Most spoilage is caused by the action of enzymes, moulds or bacteria on food; efficient canning slows or stops these agents of decomposition.

Enzymes change the chemical composition of foods. They make tomatoes redden and peaches ripen; they also cause fruits and vegetables to decompose and lose their texture, taste and colour. Heat, sugar, salt and vinegar all stop enzymes in their tracks.

Micro-organisms also spoil food. Many harmful micro-organisms can be removed by simply washing fruits and vegetables. Yeasts and moulds are slowed down considerably at 0°C; sterilization in boiling water is the only sure way to kill bacteria and molds, as some produce spores which resist freezing temperatures.

Bacteria are the most difficult micro-organisms to destroy, and are also the most deadly.

One bacterium, *Staphylococcus aureus*, is the most common cause of food poisoning in Canada. Personal cleanliness, careful washing of foodstuffs and cooking utensils, and strict adherence to recipe instructions will greatly reduce the risk of staphylococcus contamination.

Clostridium botulinum, also known as botulism, is a fearful killer. It exists in common soil in a completely harmless spore form. It produces a lethal toxin when it reproduces in food. Fortunately, adequate heat and sanitary food preparation make botulism outbreaks relatively rare.

Sterilization

All parts of a canning jar must be sterilized shortly before use. The glass pieces should first be washed with hot water and dishwashing detergent, and then rinsed. The jars should then be turned upside-down and boiled in water which rises five to six centimetres above the jar tops. Fifteen minutes of boiling is required for complete sterilization. Leave the jars in hot water until you're ready to use them. A dishwasher can be used, if it is set at the highest temperature.

An oven may also be used for sterilization. In this method, the jars should be washed and rinsed as above, and then heated in an oven at 100°C for fifteen minutes.

Some metal lids may require different sterilization methods than those described above. It is best to refer to the manufacturer's instructions when sterilizing lids.

Conversion Tables

Volume

1 L = 0.264 gal.   1 gal. = 3.785 L
      = 1.76 pt.   1 pt.   = 473 mL
      = 2.11 qt.   1 qt.   = 946 mL
      = 4.54 cups   1 cup   = 240 mL
                                    1 Tbsp = 15 mL
                                    1 tsp   = 5 mL

Weight

1 g = 0.0353 oz.   1 oz. = 28.35 g
1 kg = 2.296 lbs.   1 lb.   = 435.6 g

Length

1 cm = 0.3937"   1"   = 2.54 cm

Temperature

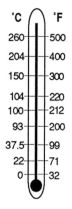

°C	°F
260	500
204	400
150	300
104	220
100	212
93	200
37.5	99
22	71
0	32

Index to Recipes